SWU-NAP- 002

POLISH SOLDIERS DURING THE NAPOLEONIC WARS

THE POLISH LEGIONS, THE ARMY OF THE DUCHY OF WARSAW AND THE POLISH IN THE GRAND ARMÉE

From the Chaelminski, B.Gembarzewski,
A.Trzeszczkowski. A. Rembowski and others
greatest artworks on the Polish soldiers

SOLDIERSHOP PUBLISHING

Title: **POLISH SOLDIERS DURING THE NAPOLEONIC WARS**
The Polish Legions, the army of Duchy of Warsaw and the Polish in the Grand Armée
Serie edit by Luca S. Cristini. First edition by Soldiershop. May 2018
Cover & Art Design: Luca S. Cristini.
ISBN code: 978-88-93273459
Published by Soldiershop publishing, via Padre Davide, 7 - 24050 Zanica (BG) ITALY. www.soldiershop.com

POLISH SOLDIERS DURING THE NAPOLEONIC WARS

THE POLISH LEGIONS,
THE ARMY OF DUCHY OF WARSAW
AND THE POLISH IN THE GRAND ARMÉE

THE POLISH SOLDIER IN NAPOLEONIC ERA

'I like the Poles'! With these words a young and then idealistic general, Napoleon Bonaparte, show at all his personal thinking in Verona (Italy) in 1797.

He finished his discourse with: *"The partition of Poland was an iniquitous deed that cannot stand. When I have finished the war in Italy I will lead the French myself and will force the Russians to re-establish Poland."*

Like all reciprocated and mutual loves, to the Poles, the image of Bonaparte was seen as that of a great hero; a liberator who lit a brief beacon of hope in the recently divided country.

We must also remember that in those years, the Napoleon's heart was also involved in the deep liason with a vivacious young Polish Countess, Marie Walewska.

Related the Polish-French friendship we remember also the words of the Polish national anthem are derived from the marching song of France's first Polish legions, which were formed under General Henryk Dabrowski in 1797: *"March, march Dabrowski, from Italy to Poland. Under your command we will reunite with the nation."*

The Polish troops were amongst the most distinguished in the Grande Armée, and over a hundred thousand of them perished fighting for the cause. Nevertheless, in terms of the recreation of a Polish kingdom, Napoleon's canny minister, Charles-Maurice de Talleyrand, advised that Poland was not worth *"a single drop of French blood."*...

In this book we present the best artwork of this romantic era. Nineteenth century oil paintings of valiant cavalry charges abound, as do portraits of proud generals, likewise the glittering uniforms of the Polish troops themselves. The most famous Polish artist of this era are Jan Chelminski, Bronislaw Gembarzewski, Jozef Brandt, Julius Kosack, Jan Alojzy Matejko and Antoni Trzeszczkowski.

◀ Prince Jozef Poniatowski in front of Polish grenadiers. Canvas by January Suchodolski (1857)

CONTENTS

*

Preface pag. 5

*

*

THE POLISH LEGIONS

The Polish Legions also known as the Dąbrowski Legions) were many Polish military units that served with the French Army during the Napoleonic wars, mainly from 1797 to 1815. The Polish Legions saw combat in most of Napoleon's campaigns, from the West Indies, through Italy and Egypt. When the Duchy of Warsaw was created in 1807, many of the veterans of the Legions formed a core around which the Duchy's army was raised under Józef Poniatowski.

This force fought a victorious war against Austria in 1809 and would go on to fight alongside the French army in numerous campaigns, culminating in the disastrous invasion of Russia in 1812, which marked the end of the Napoleonic empire, including the Legions, and allied states like the Duchy of Warsaw. The people that served under the Polish flags are about 30.000 men.

After the various partitions of Poland, many Poles believed that revolutionary France, whose public opinion was very sympathetic to the ideals of the Polish Constitution.

The France's enemies are also Polish enemies: Prussia, Austria and Imperial Russia. So, Paris becomes the seat of two Polish organizations laying the claim to be the Polish government in exile.

In the main time, many Polish soldiers, officers and volunteers therefore emigrated, especially to Italy and to France. With all this available soldier the French decided to use the Poles for first, to bolster their allies in Italy, the Cisalpine Republic. The first leader of this force was Jan Henryk Dąbrowski, a former high-ranking officer in the army of the Polish-Lithuanian confederation.

At that time, he went to Paris, and later, Milan. Dąbrowski was soon authorized by the

▲ Jan Henryk Dąbrowski, the most famous commander of the Polish Legions by J. Kossak

Italian allied of Cisalpine Republic to create the Polish Legions, which would be part of the army on 9 January 1797, and marked the formal creation of the first Polish Legions.

These Polish soldiers serving in the Dąbrowski Legion were were allowed to use their own unique Polish-style uniforms, with some French and Italian symbols. By the start of the year 1797 the Legion was 1,200 strong, having been bolstered by the arrival of many new recruits of Poles origins who had deserted from the Austrian army. The Dąbrowski Legion was first used against Austrians and their allies in Italy. In May 1797 the Legion was reorganized into two formations, each numbering about 4.000 infantry, and men of artillery support. After the Treaty of Campo Formio, In May 1798 the Poles helped the French to secure the Papal States, putting down some peasant revolts, and garrisoned Rome, which they entered on 3 May.

After this first battles, the Polish soldiers fought in the War of the Second Coalition, always on Italian front but later also on German front. In 1802 France sent most of the Polish legionnaires (about 5,000 men) to Haiti to put down the Haitian Revolution.

The Haitian campaign proved the first disastrous for the legionnaires. Combat casualties and tropical diseases, including the yellow fever, reduced the strong Polish contingent to a few hundred survivors in short time. The Polish were present also in the Wars of the Third and Fourth Coalition of 1805 and 1806. And finally, after the creation of the Duchy of Warsaw born the famous Vistula Legion, On 31 March 1808. The Vistula Legion had a strength of 6,000.

During the Peninsular War (1809–1814) in Spain, the Vistula Legion gained fame at the Battle of Zaragoza. Other troops served in Napoleon's Imperial Guard and the Polish Chevau-léger regiment distinguished itself at the Battle of Somosierra in 1808.

Another Polish cavalry regiment – the Vistula uhlans – also fought in Spain.

THE RUSSIAN WAR OF 1812 AND THE END

When Napoleon entered Russia, the Poles and Lithuanians rallied to Napoleon's Grande Armée in the hope of resurrecting the Poles state. The Vistula Legion, return from Spain in early 1812 and reorganized into a division. For the Russian campaign, the Poles formed the largest foreign contingent, 100,000 men about (the entire French Grande Armée was about 600,000 strong). They distinguished in the Battle of Borodino and, under Prince

▲ The entry in Rome of the Polish general Jan Henryk Dąbrowski ib a paint of January_Suchodolski_

◄ A polish hussar trumpet by Bronislaw Gembarzewski

Józef Poniatowski (who personally saved Napoleon's life), were one of the units that served as the rear guard during Napoleon's retreat. At the end of this disastrous war only 26,000 of the original 98,000-strong Polish contingent returned. For sample the Vistula Legion entering Russia was about 7,000 strong; its strength at the end of the campaign was just 1,500.

The definitive end of the Polish Legions came with the conclusion of Napoleon's career and the abolition of the Duchy of Warsaw. The Duchy was occupied by Prussian and Russian troops following Napoleon's retreat from Russia. After Napoleon's defeat in the War of the Sixth Coalition, when Napoleon was forced into exile on Elba, the only unit he was allowed to keep as guards were the Polish Lancers. Later some hundreds of Polish participating in the Battle of Waterloo.

DUCHY OF WARSAW

Was one of the most famous Client state of the French Empire and Personal union with the Kingdom of Saxony with capital Warsaw. The state extended for about 100.000 km² With a population of about 4.500.000 in the 1809. The Duchy of Warsaw was established by Napoleon I in 1807 from the Polish lands ceded by the Kingdom of Prussia under the terms of the Treaties of Tilsit. The duchy was held in personal union by one of Napoleon's allies, King Frederick Augustus I of Saxony. Following Napoleon's failed invasion of Russia, the duchy was occupied by Prussian and Russian troops until 1815, when it was formally partitioned between the two countries at the Congress of Vienna. The duchy's armed forces were completely under French control via its war minister, Prince Józef Poniatowski, who was also a Marshal of France. In fact, the duchy was heavily militarized, bordered as it was by Prussia, the Austrian Empire, and Russia, and it was to be a significant source for troops in various campaigns of Napoleon.

▲ Prince Józef Poniatowski Commander in Chief of forces of Duchy of Warsaw, by Juliusz Kossak   ► Map of the Duchy of Warsaw in 1809

ARMY OF THE DUCHY OF WARSAW

The Army was significantly based on the Polish Legions; it numbered about 30,000 and was expanded during wartime to almost 100,000 on a state population of 2,6 milion of people.
So the size of the army was a considerable economic burden to the small state. It was composed of infantry with a strong cavalry force supported by artillery. The Napoleonic customs and traditions resulted in some social tensions, but are generally credited with helpful modernization and useful reforms. The great part of the Army of the Duchy of Warsaw was formed by the oldest legionnaires of the Polish Legions. In addition, after his creation it was filled by soldiers from the Army of the Polish–Lithuanian union, who responded to the call to arms of Józef Poniatowski. The army was expanded several times during his life and it was doubled in 1809.
Several regiments were sponsored by the French and for the Russian war of 1812, almost 100,000 men were roled. It is estimated that about 180,000 to 200,000 men served in the Army throughout its brief existence.

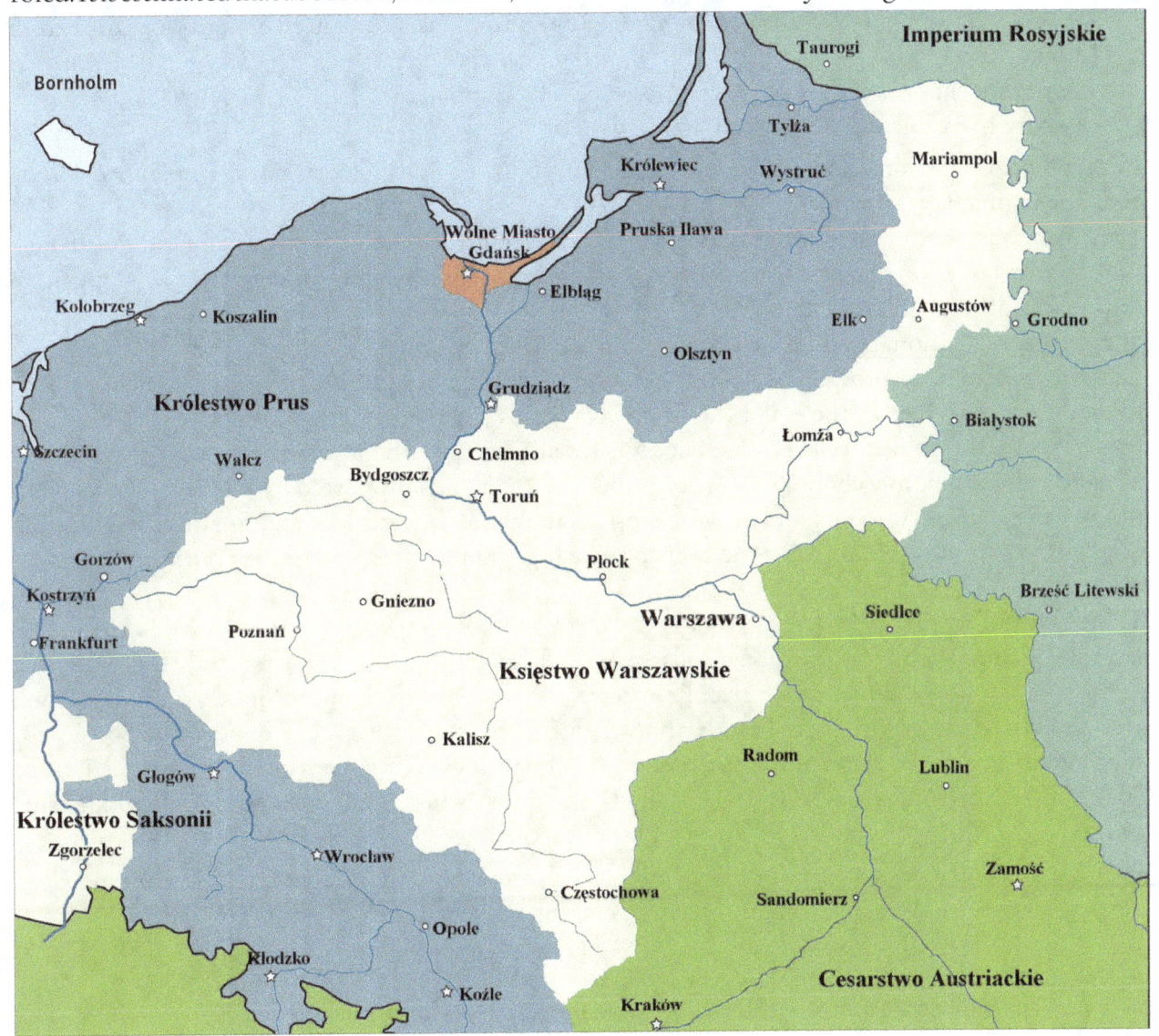

In addition to the Army of the Duchy of Warsaw, Poles also served in other formations allied to France; most notably, the Vistula Legion (see before).

In addition to the standing army, a national guard could be called into action in 1809 and 1811. The most famous and notable Polish commanders of the Army of the Duchy of Warsaw was the Prince Józef Poniatowski (who was the army chief commander throughout most of its history) and the general Jan Henryk Dąbrowski.

The Army of the Duchy of Warsaw was composed of the following formations (the number refer to his organization in the Imperial Napoleonic army):
- one regiment of cuirassiers (14th)
- ten regiments of uhlan lancers (2nd, 3rd, 6th, 7th, 8th, 9th, 11th, 12th, 15th, 16th); five more were
- formed in Lithuania in 1812
- two regiments of hussars (10th and 13th)
- three regiments of chasseurs (1st, 4th and 5th)-
- seventeen regiments of infantry (numbered one through seventeen; five more were formed in Lithuania in 1812)
- one regiment of horse artillery (composed of four companies)
- twenty five companies of regular artillery

In 1813 several units of light cavalry, the Krakusi (Cracus, or Polish cossacks), were planned; in the end, one regiment was formed.

The Army was the site of a cultural clash of new, democratic French traditions and old Polish customs, with clashes on the role of nobility in the military – with some conservatives attempting to restrict the officer rank to the nobles.

The French revolutionary and civic traditions, passed through veteran legionnaires.

The army was also improved due to the modernization and adoption of modern French military rules and tactics. Overall, the era of the Duchy of Warsaw marked a period of modernization of the Polish Army. The obligatory time of service was set at 6 years, with any citizens aged 21 to 28 having a chance to be randomly chosen for conscription. The Army was supported by the new schools, with the 3-year Elementary School and a 1-year Applicant School for Artillery and Engineering. Overall, the Polish units were reckoned by the French to be highly motivated and of high quality.

THE ARTISTS

Jan van Chelminski (1851–1925), great Polish painter, born in Brzustów. His first study was under the famous Juliusz Kossak in Warsaw. After he entered the Munich Academy of Fine Arts on 1875. Note also his collaboration with Józef Brandt. In 1897, during his stay in Paris, he founded the Society for the Care of Polish Art After the artist becomes an English citizen and worked throughout Europe and lived in New York from 1895. He was best known in his lifetime for his historical works, especially those dealing with military history and the Napoleonic Wars.

Bronisław Gembarzewski (1872-1941) - painter, war historian, military historian, museum manager, director of the National Museum in 1916-1936, creator of the Military Museum in Warsaw.

- ► **3** Sketch of Polish lancer in high dress by Bronisław Gembarzewski.
- ► at pag. 14: Staff of the Duchy of Warsaw." by Antoni Trzeszczkowski.

P.M. 2.VI. 1928.

THE
COLOUR
PLATES

FROM THE WORK OF JAN CHELMINSKI

General commander the Prince Joseph Poniatowsi

General ADC of Major Staff

Officers of hussars, grenadiers, fusiliers,, lancers and mounted Jaeger

Brigade ADC

8th lancers regiment

5th infantry regiment

11th lancers regiment

ADC of Poniatowki

Medical corps, surgeon and veterinaries

Officer of foot artillery

Drums major of 13th, 1st and national guard

7th Vistula lancers in Spain

Prince Poniatowski's guide

28

Staff of military school of artillery and engineer

10th hussar regiment

Officer of horse artillery

General of brigade in service dress, lancers colonel and voltigeur

Brigade general, colonel, officer and veteran troops

16th lancer elite company

Engineer corps: private and officer

ADC division and 7th lancer officer

trumpets of cuirassier and horse artillery

Military school of artillery and engineer

3rd lancer regiment

Military train and war commissariat officer

Foot artillery

Officer of lancers in great uniforms (1st formation)

Vistula legion: sapper, cornet, drummer and soldiers

2nd infantry regiment and vivandiere

14th cuirassier

8th regiment of Vistula lancers in winter dress

46

5th regiment of mounted Jaeger

Artilleryman, Jaeger, cuirassier and lancers in service dress

4th mounted Jaeger

Polish imperial guard lancer timbalier

Company of lancers in the Elba island

8th infantry regiment at the battle of Raszyn

Trumpets of the 2nd lancers

Officer and soldiers of Polish krakus

Voltigeurs of Vistula legion

Gendarmerie: Marshall of logis

Trumpet of 13th hussar and officer of 1st mounted jager

12th infantry regiment at Beresina battle

Commander in the holidays dress

Officer at military review

Grenadier of national guard and officer

Lithuanian tartars

Lancer of Imperial Guard

Officer of Polish lancers of the Imperial Guard

Napoleon and his staff

NAPOLÉON Iᵉʳ

Empereur des Français

FRÉDÉRIC-AUGUSTE

Roi de Saxe, Duc de Varsovie

JERZMANOWSKI

A. SKARZYNSKI

Cte ZAMOYSKI

SZYMANOWSKI

Gal KNIAZIEWICZ

Pce ROMUALD GIEDROYC

LONCZYNSKI

Cte CZACKI

Cte PAC

WEYSSENHOFF

K. DOMAŃSKI

Flag of 1st Polish regiment of chasseur at horse

Eaglrs of 10 Infantry reg. (1), 11 reg. (2), 13 reg. (3) and eagle of Polish flag (4)

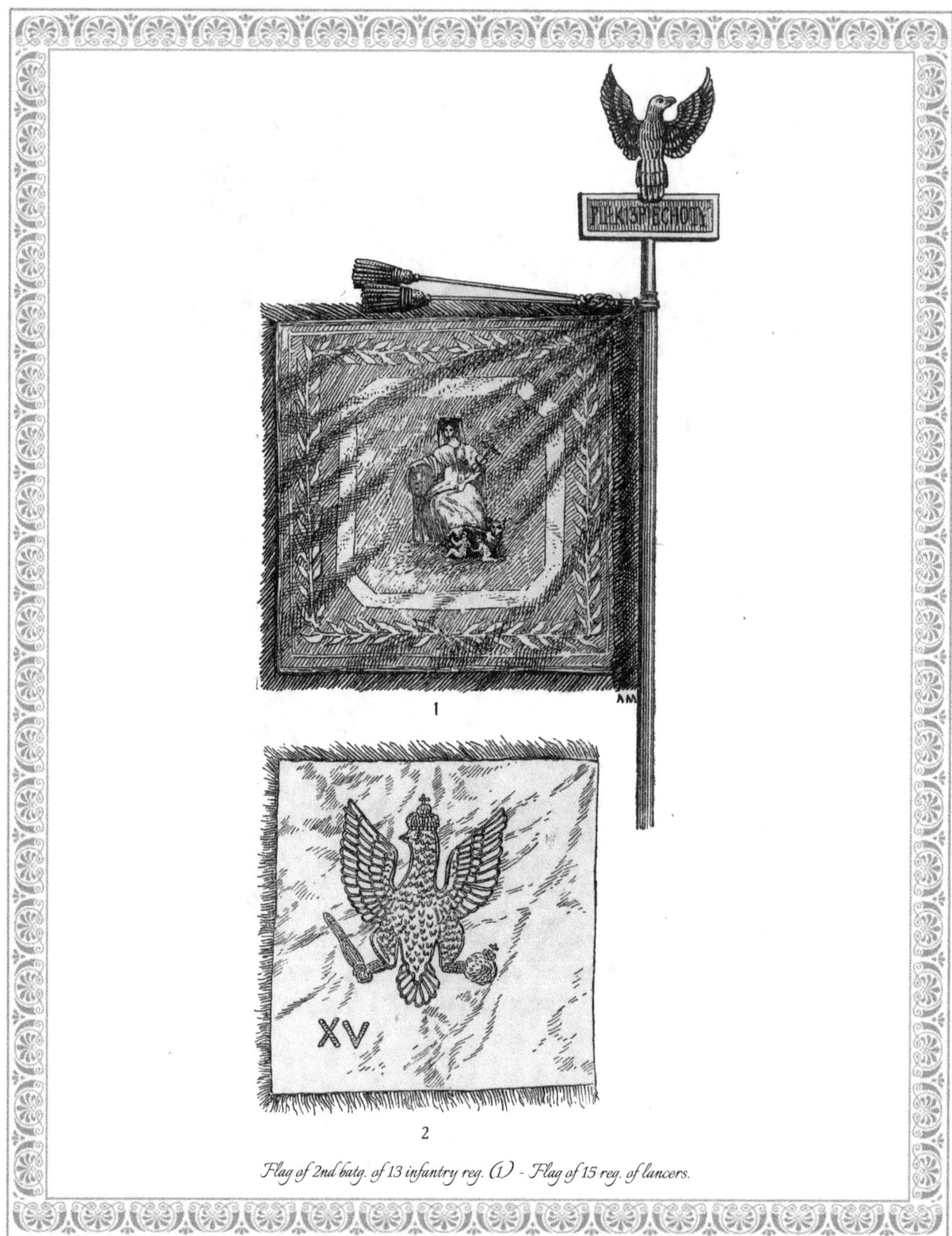

Flag of 2nd batg. of 13 infantry reg. (1) - Flag of 15 reg. of lancers.

Fanion of 1st regiment of Polish Chevau legers of Imperial Guard

POLISH LANCERS
OF THE
IMPERIAL GUARD

FROM THE WORK OF ALEXANDRE REMBOVSKI

High officer in great uniforms

Imperial lancer of the Guard

Officer and trumpet in campaign dress

Lancer in campaign dress

Lancers timbalier in high dress

Lancer trumpet in high dress

Lithuanian tartars

Lancer in winter dress with mantel

NCOs in high dress and in sortout

Officers in service dress, in high uniforms, on the back soldiers in service dress

POLISH ARMY

1807-1830

FROM THE WORK OF BRONISLAW GEMBARZEWSKI

1808 General Dywizyi

1810 Cuirassier high officer

1812 Polish hulans in review

1812 Polish mounted jager

1809 infantry regiment

1809 10th Polish hussars

1809 Horse artillery

1814 Polish krakus

1816 Polish general

1815-1826 Grenadier Guards

1828-1830 1st Polish foot chasseur

1815-1822 Chasseur at horse

1822 Standard bearer of Polish hulans

1815-1824 2nd Polish hulans regiment

1822-1824 Polish horse artillery

1815-1828 Gendarme at horse

SOLDIERS, WEAPONS & UNIFORMS ALREADY PUBLISHED
(SELECTION TITLES)

UNIFORMS OF RUSSIAN ARMY IN THE ERA OF ANCIENT TZAR
FROM THE REIGN OF VASILI IV TO MICHAEL I, ALEXIS, FEODOR III DURING THE XVII th CENTURY
A.V.VISKOVATOV   LUCA STEFANO CRISTINI
SWU-600-004

UNIFORMS OF RUSSIAN ARMY OF PETER I THE GREAT
FROM THE REIGN OF PETER I TO CATHERINE I, PEER II, ANNA AND IVAN VI. 1682-1741
A.V.VISKOVATOV   LUCA STEFANO CRISTINI
SWU-700-006

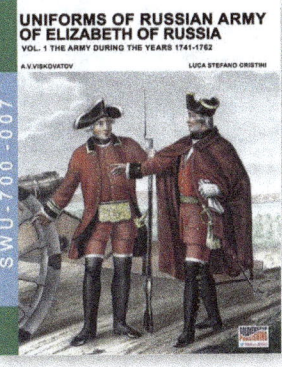

UNIFORMS OF RUSSIAN ARMY OF ELIZABETH OF RUSSIA
VOL. 1 THE ARMY DURING THE YEARS 1741-1762
A.V.VISKOVATOV   LUCA STEFANO CRISTINI
SWU-700-007

UNIFORMS OF RUSSIAN ARMY OF ELIZABETH OF RUSSIA
VOL. 2 THE ARMY DURING THE YEARS 1741-1762
A.V.VISKOVATOV   LUCA STEFANO CRISTINI
SWU-700-008

UNIFORMS OF RUSSIAN ARMY IN THE XVIII CENTURY VOL. 1
UNDER THE REIGN OF CATHERINE II EMPRESS OF RUSSIA BETWEEN 1762 AND 1796
A.V.VISKOVATOV - LUCA STEFANO CRISTINI
SWU-700-005

UNIFORMS OF RUSSIAN ARMY IN THE XVIII CENTURY VOL. 2
UNDER THE REIGN OF CATHERINE II EMPRESS OF RUSSIA BETWEEN 1762 AND 1796
A.V.VISKOVATOV - LUCA STEFANO CRISTINI
SWU-700-009

UNIFORMS OF RUSSIAN ARMY IN THE XVIII CENTURY VOL. 3
UNDER THE REIGN OF CATHERINE II EMPRESS OF RUSSIA BETWEEN 1762 AND 1796
A.V.VISKOVATOV - LUCA STEFANO CRISTINI
SWU-700-010

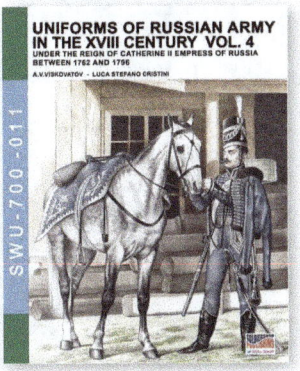

UNIFORMS OF RUSSIAN ARMY IN THE XVIII CENTURY VOL. 4
UNDER THE REIGN OF CATHERINE II EMPRESS OF RUSSIA BETWEEN 1762 AND 1796
A.V.VISKOVATOV - LUCA STEFANO CRISTINI
SWU-700-011

BRITISH ARMY UNIFORMS IN 1742
IN THE ART OF JOHN PINE
SWU-700-001

UNIFORMS OF RUSSIAN ARMY OF ELIZABETH OF RUSSIA
VOL. 2 THE ARMY DURING THE YEARS 1741-1762
A.V.VISKOVATOV   LUCA STEFANO CRISTINI
SWU-700-008

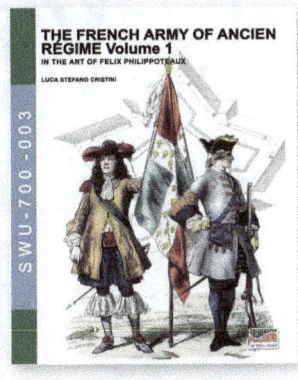

THE FRENCH ARMY OF ANCIEN RÉGIME Volume 1
IN THE ART OF FELIX PHILIPPOTEAUX
LUCA STEFANO CRISTINI
SWU-700-003

THE FRENCH ARMY OF ANCIEN RÉGIME Volume 2
IN THE ART OF FELIX PHILIPPOTEAUX
LUCA STEFANO CRISTINI
SWU-700-004

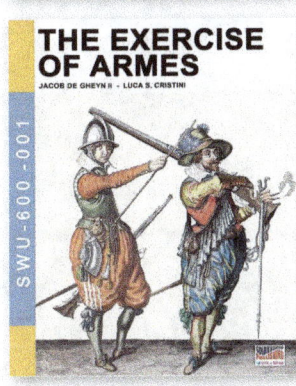

THE EXERCISE OF ARMES
JACOB DE GHEYN II - LUCA S. CRISTINI
SWU-600-001

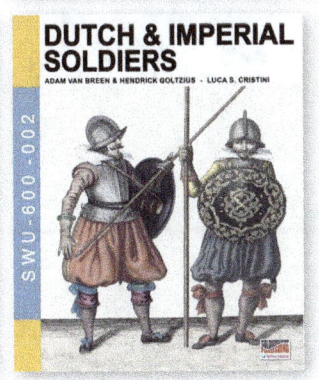

DUTCH & IMPERIAL SOLDIERS
ADAM VAN BREEN & HENDRICK GOLTZIUS - LUCA S. CRISTINI
SWU-600-002

HORSEMEN IN THE 16TH & 17TH C.
JACOB DE GHEYN II - A.DE BRUYN - LUCA S. CRISTINI
SWU-600-003

IMPERIAL SOLDIERS & UNIFORMS 1640-1860
IN THE ART OF FRANZ GERASCH
LUCA S. CRISTINI   Plates by FRANZ GERASCH
SWU-GEN-001